APPLIQUÉ ALPHABET

For Marjorie Jean
with love and thanks.

APPLIQUÉ ALPHABET

FRUIT AND FLOWER LETTER DESIGNS
FOR YOU TO MAKE

STEWART MERRETT

B. T. BATSFORD

ACKNOWLEDGMENT
The lyric on page 37 of this book is produced by kind permission of the Williamson Music Company,
NY, USA. Copyright © 1959 by Richard Rodgers and Oscar Hammerstein II. Copyright Renewed.
WILLIAMSON MUSIC owner of publication and allied rights throughout the world.
International Copyright Secured. Used by Permission. All Rights Reserved.

First published in Great Britain by B. T. Batsford Ltd.
4 Fitzhardinge Street, London W1H OAH

Created and produced by The Watermark Press, Sydney
Text copyright © Stewart Merrett 1994
Appliqué designs copyright © Stewart Merrett 1994
This compilation copyright © The Watermark Press, 1994

Editor: Diane Wallis
Designer: Linda Soo
Photography: Simon Blackall
Styling: Babette Hayes
Research: Sheelagh Callaghan
Printed and bound by Kyodo Printing, Singapore

A catalogue record for this book is available from the British Library
ISBN 0 7134 7460 2

CONTENTS

INTRODUCTION

A is for apple, B is for ball, C is for cat. Images spring to mind the moment a letter of the alphabet is presented. We relate our own personal imagery to each particular symbol of language because this is how we were taught to remember them.

This book is a collection of twenty-six images and designs that are historic symbols of my native tongue and its alphabet, the Roman alphabet, which is used in most countries of the Western world. As well as many other languages with the same or similar alphabet there are many other alphabets, but fortunately I am not familiar with them or this book would never have been finished.

In selecting the images I found it necessary to limit the choice of decorative or illuminated letters to fruit, flowers and the odd vegetable and plant. To do otherwise would have made the task impossible. After all, C is for crocus, camel, cathedral or cockerel. The choice is endless.

Once having made my choice it became necessary to research the various plants and flowers in the collection. I was keen to have a whimsical mix of colour with the odd surprise such as T for turnip, just to keep you guessing. Along the way I discovered that many of the illustrated alphabeticals completely ignored the letter U because it was just too

Opposite: Relaxing with the V-for-violet cushion in my courtyard. Above: The red version of A for apple.

hard. And it is – very! My letter U is for the umbrella tree *Schefflera actinophylla*, which only looks at its best in a rainforest. Fortunately the leaf form of this rather all-pervading tree lends itself superbly to its Roman letter.

Another nightmarish selection was for the letter X. In desperation I switched from the unfortunate name of 'blackboy' to the botanical *Xanthorrhea*, which I am sure is nowhere near the tip of even the most dedicated gardener's tongue. Hopefully, the exposure of the correct name in this book will play some small part in the demise of the old, colonial name. This unique shrub, which is native to my home state,

is currently the subject of major research; in time its pre-historic secrets may be revealed.

The real favourites of course are 'the pretties': the violets, daffodils and roses. The selection seemed simple at the time of planning but there were still executive choices to be made! Should it be D for daffodil, daisy, daphne or dahlia? The final choice became personal, based on what I thought would work best in appliqué and enhance the alphabet as a whole. The process was fairly exhausting so no correspondence will be entered into.

The cushion application of the illuminated letters seemed to be the simplest and most appropriate use for these designs. This size of work is not daunting and the finished pieces can be comfortably absorbed into your domestic environment to be admired and coveted by everyone. One of the great things about the textile arts is their ability to be part of our day to day lives and not just admired in a glass case. Having said that I would still like to encourage you to be adventurous and make the designs as large as one metre (three feet) square to stretch over frames for use as wall panels. Even at my suggested cushion scale, they all work well as small wall pieces or could be used as the side panels of a 'carpet bag'. You may prefer to have the image the same size as it appears on the pages of this book and use very delicate fabrics for the appliqué for exquisitely initialed patch pockets.

I think it is always important to approach work like this with a 'devil may care' attitude and certainly not as a tense traditional-

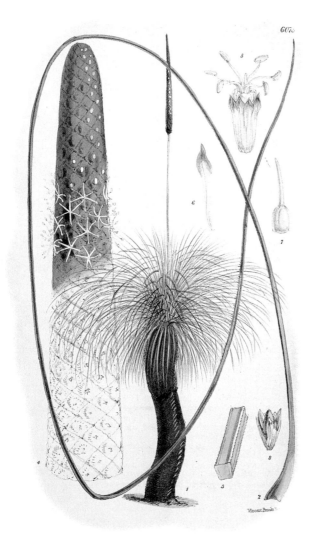

The Xanthorrhea *fascinated professional and amateur botanists in the early days of white settlement in Australia.*

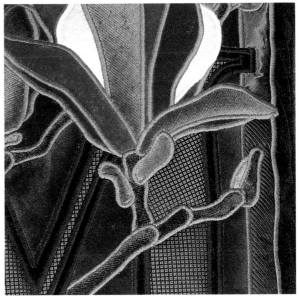

Above: *I store colour-grouped fabrics in clear plastic bags*. Above right: *Close-up of tie fabrics in M cushion*. Right: *Stitching detail from U*.

ist who believes that pursed lips lead to perfection. The back of your work can be chaos – no one will ever know unless you insist on confessing to the stitch police.

Attack this work with verve, pleasure and even an element of risk, selecting outlandish colour combinations that may not work in the conventional sense. The designs are all sound and if your daffodils are blue and brown and the threads you choose are purple and green, the stitching should bring the finished piece together.

The secret of the appeal of the work is the mix of textiles which will yield a rich and textured surface. If you make a mistake, only you will know. Leave it in and the rest of the world will think it is an integral part of your masterpiece. Do not worry if your sewing is a bit wobbly or you lose concentration on a dangerous corner. It is important that you show the struggle.

My ultimate fantasy for these decorative letters is that you will make enough of them to spell out something deep and meaningful so that by chance an inquisitive visitor may be confronted with more than just exquisite appliqué.

MACHINE APPLIQUÉ TECHNIQUE

At first, my technique looks complicated with its many different and seemingly mysterious steps but accuracy and stability are the reasons for this. Read through this part of the text, follow the step-by-step illustrations on pages 16 – 19 carefully and when you attempt your first piece of machine appliqué you will be rewarded by success.

The design is traced onto *two* pieces of calico. One is pinned to a pin board to become the placement pattern while the other is cut up into the design's shapes and then pinned on the placement pattern.

Select fabrics to be the appliqué pieces, decide on the allocation of colours and then remove the pinned-on calico pieces systematically in batches, attaching them with spray adhesive to the backs of your chosen fabrics – *one colour at a time*. Work at this process of elimination until the placement pattern is clear of pinned-on pieces. Iron the pieces flat on the back of the fabric with a warm iron and then cut out the shapes, which will then resemble jigsaw pieces.

To avoid confusion, keep colour groups in separate piles. Spray the calico side of

Opposite: *I work on a small scale, firstly on tracing paper (a personal choice – any paper will do) and then I trace the design onto acetate.* Above: *You will need two copies of the design on calico, one to be attached to the pin board as the placement pattern and the other to be cut into pieces and pinned into position on the uncut version.*

EQUIPMENT & MATERIALS
Tracing paper
Pencil
Ruler and set square
(if enlarging by hand)
Carbon paper
Calico
Scissors
Pins
Spray adhesive
Protective mask
Newspapers
Homemade spray booth
(see below)
Selection of fabric scraps
Machine threads

these jigsaw pieces with adhesive before placing them on the placement pattern. Wear a mask while using spray adhesive and work in a well-ventilated room. You can make a collapsible spray booth with three pieces of cardboard, hinged together with masking tape to form the back and sides. Protect your table surface with sheets of newspaper.

Once the jigsaw puzzle has been completed, remove it from the pin board, spray its back with adhesive and stick it to a piece of Dacron batting. Trim the assembly to the edge of the design, spray its back with adhesive and press onto the background fabric, which should be large enough to provide a 10 cm (4 in) border all round.

Machine-satin-stitch will clamp all the layers together, add the distinctive outline and accentuate the padding. Stitch the background first, the foreground last.

I do lots of machine appliqué and therefore use large quantities of sewing thread.

Recently I discovered 'bobbin-fill', which comes on a large spool. Now I use this exclusively for the underside of the work because it is much less expensive than the coloured and metallic threads I favour. The colour element comes only from the top of the sewing machine. Do not concern yourself with how the back of your sewn work looks.

Keep the colour changes of thread to a minimum. In works of the size illustrated throughout this book, use a maximum of four or five, but two or three changes would be more preferable. Different coloured elements of an appliqué design actually appear more complex when satin stitched in one colour; a happy case of the easiest option looking the most intricate.

The appliqués in this book were used on cushion covers for 50 cm (20 in) cushion fillers. The cushions were made with thick piping trim and a zipper opening set between one edge of the back and the piping. However, the designs could be stretched on panels and used as wall decoration, framed or unframed.

A more ambitious project would be a bedspread or quilt cover with nine letters, joined together in a square configuration with strips of fabric 10 centimetres (4 inches) wide with plain fabric for the side and end drops.

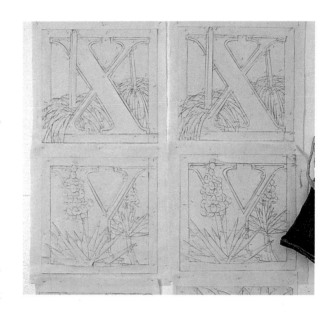

Top: *Four patterns at the pinned-on stage.*
Bottom: *The jigsaw puzzles are complete and ready
to be backed with Dacron batting.*

ENLARGING THE DESIGN

I use an overhead projector to enlarge my
appliqué images, which are drawn in black ink
onto a small sheet of acetate. As many craft
clubs, businesses, schools, colleges and organi-
zations are equipped with overhead projectors,
they are not difficult to source.

Using a piece of acetate (clear plastic
sheeting) and a black pen, trace the design and
project it on the wall onto a piece of tracing
paper. Then draw the design onto the tracing
paper with a pencil. Remove the tracing from
the wall and place it over a four-tier 'sandwich'
made up of two pieces of calico and two sheets
of carbon paper, starting at the bottom with
calico. Draw over the design again so that the
design is transferred to the two pieces of calico.

For the initial tracing of the image
from the projector and subsequent steps in
assembling the appliqué, I converted a wall of
my studio into a giant pin board by lining it
with sheets of polystyrene foam.

Without access to an overhead projector, designs can be enlarged by photocopier or
by scaling up the diagrams as they appear here.
If using a photocopier, cut the design in half
and enlarge each half separately; the finished
pattern is wider than an A3 sheet of paper.

When scaling up by hand use a set
square and ruler to draw a grid to the recom-
mended measurement using the scale of 1
square equals 2.5 cm or 1 in. To transfer the
design to this grid, mark the places on it which
correspond to where the design lines intersect
the grid. Connect these marks using a ruler for
straight lines and drawing the curves by hand.

This master pattern can now be used
for tracing two copies of the design with two
sheets of carbon paper layered alternately with
two pieces of calico.

1. *Following the instruction on page 15, enlarge the pattern. O for orchid is being enlarged here.*

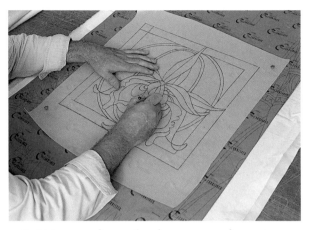

2. *Using two sheets of carbon paper and two pieces of calico, trace two copies of the pattern.*

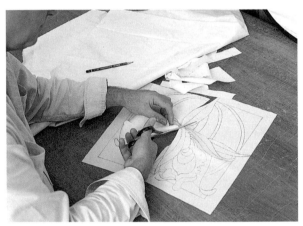

3. *Following the design lines cut one copy of the pattern into pieces and pin the other (the placement pattern) on the pin board.*

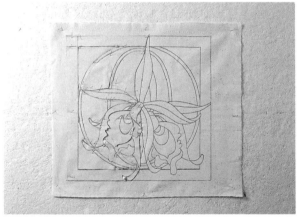

4. *Matching shapes, begin pinning the cut out pieces of calico onto placement pattern.*

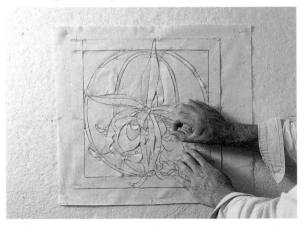

5. *Pinning on the cut out calico pieces is now complete.*

6. *Make a selection of fabrics for the appliqué.*

7. Select those calico pieces that are to be the same colour and remove from placement pattern. Do only one colour at a time to avoid confusion.

8. In a well-ventilated room, place them right side up on a table protected by newspaper and spray with adhesive while wearing a face mask.

9. Place sticky side down on wrong side of fabric, then press with a warm iron.

10. Selected fabrics are now backed with calico pieces.

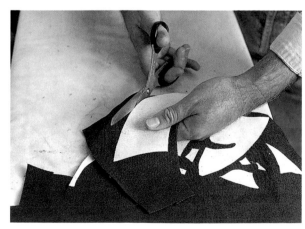

11. Now cut out the jigsaw pieces.

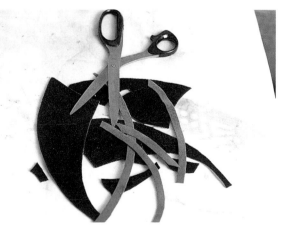

12. I started with the purple parts of the 'O' and its pink border.

13. On newspaper, place the selected jigsaw pieces face down and thoroughly cover their calico backs with spray adhesive.

14. Then begin the process of doing the jigsaw puzzle, pressing the pieces firmly onto the placement pattern. In this case I started with the broad sections of the 'O'.

15. Then added its brilliant outer border.

16. Most of background is in place.

17. The jigsaw puzzle is complete.

18. Remove the assembly from the pin board, turn it over and spray its calico back with adhesive.

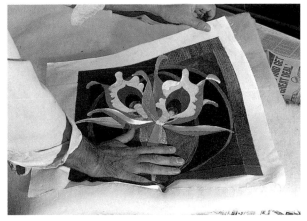

19. *Press the sticky side down onto a piece of Dacron batting the same size as·the assembly.*

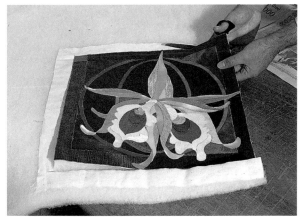

20. *Trim around the edge of the design.*

21. *Turn the assembly over and spray the back of the Dacron with adhesive.*

22. *Turn it over to the right side and press the assembly with its Dacron backing onto the background fabric.*

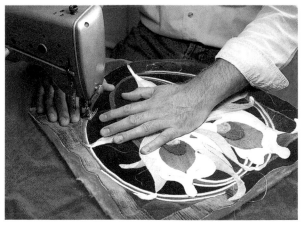

23. *Satin stitch through all layers starting with the background sections.*

24. *The pink border of the 'O' is stitched in silver metallic thread.*

A is for apple, the forbidden fruit of the Garden of Eden and a traditional image for those who speak English. The Book of Genesis makes no specific mention of apples and refers only to fruit trees but to deny Eve's legendary lure would distress countless institutions. Legend also has it that William Tell, champion of the Swiss, was forced by the Austrian governor of his canton to shoot an apple from the head of his son with a bow and arrow. The arrow found its mark without harm to the boy but even so, Tell was jailed for objecting to foreign rule. Similar events involving arrows, apples and sons are recorded in Norse legends.

Being struck on the head by an apple is said to have led Sir Isaac Newton to the discovery of gravity. Voltaire claimed to have heard this tale from Newton's niece, a certain Mrs Conduit, whose curious surname gives rise to some doubts about the story.

Today, apples have cast aside their history-making rôle. They are still widely used in cooking and one of the most famous recipes is Tarte Tatin, baked upside down with the fruit on the bottom and pastry on top, but turned over the right way when served. Created by the Demoiselles Tatin at the beginning of the century in their hotel in Sologne in western France, the dish has become so popular that deep heavy copper Tatin tins are sold especially for the cooking of this simple but delicious dessert.

But apples are not just for cooking. Eaten raw in the ratio of one a day they are purported to keep the doctor away. They are also fermented to make cider, distilled to make apple brandy, and pigs love them!

One square = 2.5 centimetres (1 inch)

WORKING NOTES: To accentuate the gold letter and its deeper gold surround, I used gold metallic thread; this gold-on-gold formula never fails. The background blue makes the obvious sky and apple grove connection. You can manipulate the nap of cloth to produce interesting variations for shapes assigned the same colour by putting the calico shapes down at random on the back of cloth. This always works and is always a pleasant surprise. The other colour way is an exercise in high contrast with bright red apples against green.

b is for banksia, named after Sir Joseph Banks, a brilliant young English botanist who sailed the world with Captain James Cook and landed in Australia in 1770. Banks was entranced by the multitude of new species he found in Australia, and it was these discoveries which helped propel him to the forefront of botanical studies in England.

There are no soft petals on the banksia flower which is more like a bottlebrush than a garden bloom. So successfully does the banksia cope with its harsh natural habitat that, when cultivated, special steps must be taken to ensure propagation of seeds. In the wild, the banksia willingly drops seeds from its cones after bushfires. A homegrown banksia's cones usually have to be baked in the oven for an hour before they will split open and release their seeds.

Another native of England who was intrigued by the native plants in her new land, was May Gibbs, who wrote and illustrated the Australian children's classic *Snugglepot and Cuddlepie* in 1918. In her tale, the innocent gumnut babies Snugglepot and Cuddlepie are continually terrorised by the big bad banksia men (probably a product of *Banksia serrata*), who take their threatening form from the distinctive cones used as the basis for my design for the letter B.

One square = 2.5 centimetres (1 inch)

WORKING NOTES: Not the banksia flower (too difficult to interpret in a broad appliqué technique) but the woody seed cone. Foliage can range from pale dusty grey-green to vivid green, charred black or bleached white depending on the variety, time of year and bushfire damage. At left, the thread for the B is multi-coloured silver moiré, which goes with anything and here heightens the contrast between the letter and its purple borders. Cones in the green version are purple, blue and charcoal and the B is stitched in metallic gold.

*Naked they came to that smooth-swarded bower,
and at their feet the crocus brake like fire.*

ALFRED LORD TENNYSON

C is for crocus, the first sign of winter's end. These small cheerful flowers may be blue, white, yellow, bright orange, lilac or purple.

The most famous member of the crocus family is *Crocus sativus*, the saffron crocus. It takes around 50,000 stigmas to produce 100g of saffron, each stigma being extracted by hand and then dried. Could this be the most expensive spice in the world?

Until the Middle Ages, saffron was a widely used ingredient for cooking, magic and medicine. Around 1785, the word 'crocus' was commonly used to refer to a quack doctor and 'crocused' to describe the treatment received at the hands of such a practitioner.

During the Renaissance, Italian women used this spice to colour their hair. Fabrics were also dyed with saffron to produce golden hues, and today the Buddhist monks of southern Asia are still clothed in saffron coloured robes.

Saffron is rarer these days and is most likely to be found in the kitchen for flavouring such dishes as bouillabaisse, paella and risotto.

Horticulture is no haven from fashion and crocus flowers, for so long the poor relation of the the many flashy varieties of spring bulbs, are enjoying a revival. The current Duke of Devonshire is a great crocus enthusiast and claims to have once had seventy two varieties in bloom between January and April.

WORKING NOTES: These are what I call Barbara Cartland colours; an overlay of lush, plush pastels with pink on pink on cream on white. The crocus was worked with a selection of white fabrics – satin, silk, moiré taffeta and a creamy shantung. To extend the theme, it was stitched with dead white cotton. Yellow stamens stitched in gold are the only highlight. Further gentle contrast comes from sage-green leaves and the dusty pink letter. Dark green leaves of the yellow crocus (left) were the inspiration for this colour change.

d is for daffodil, a bloom much admired by poets, writers, gardeners and flower fanciers. The name daffodil is a corruption of the mythical flower asphodel, which grew on the graves along the banks of the Acheron, the river of the Underworld. The botanical name for daffodil is *Narcissus*, after the beautiful youth who fell in love with his own reflection in the water of a fountain and died of despair.

Many authors have used daffodils in their works and few more effectively than Shakespeare. As he writes fondly in *The Winter's Tale* 'Daffodils, / That come before the swallow dares, and take / The winds of March with beauty'. Perhaps daffodils have no finer champion in verse than Wordsworth who wrote in his Grasmere journal 'I never saw daffodils so beautiful. They ... tossed and reeled and danced, and seemed as if they verily laughed with the wind that blew upon them over the lake'.

Daffodils are scented, and the medium and small cupped varieties are more inclined to have a rich, sweet smell. The shallow cup of the daffodil is an adaptation that makes it easier for the flower to be pollinated as the strong perfume both attracts and guides insects.

So popular has the daffodil become that today there are over 8000 named varieties.

FLORAL WARNING

Daffodils don't mix with other cut flowers. Their stems secrete substances which are detrimental to other blooms.

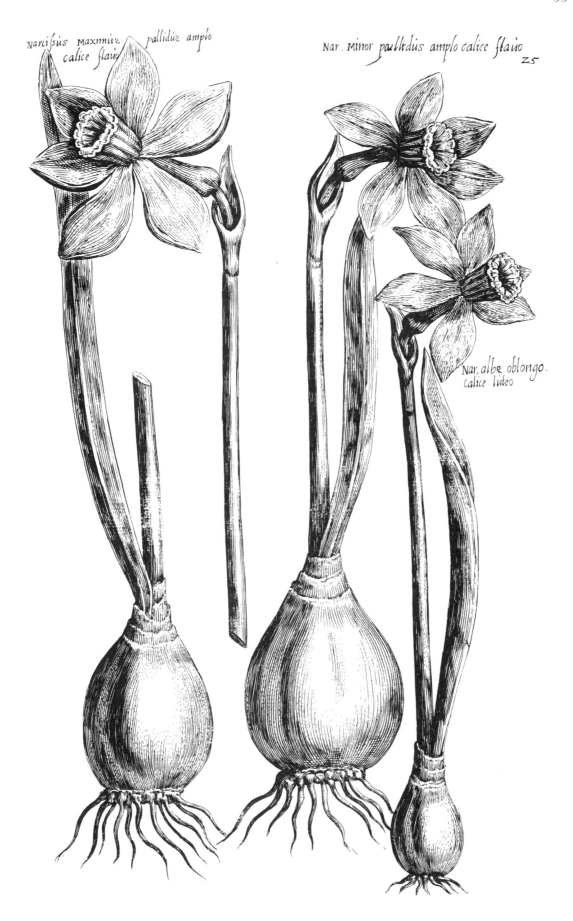

Narcissus maximus pallidus amplo
calice flauo

Nar. minor pallidus amplo calice flauo
25

Nar. albe oblongo.
calice luteo

WORKING NOTES: The many slender pieces for leaves and stems make this the most complicated design in the whole collection. To attempt this one you need great patience at the construction (jigsaw puzzle) stage. The actual sewing is less taxing. Lightweight fabrics break down when a design calls for lots of over-sewing so here I used tough velvet. The letter D is practically hidden so I outlined it in gold for emphasis. In the other one I made the flowers white, but you don't have to be botanically correct. Make them pink if you want to.

Edelweiss, edelweiss
Every morning you greet me
Small and white, clean and bright
You look happy to greet me.
Blossom of snow may you bloom and grow,
Bloom and grow forever.
Edelweiss, edelweiss
Bless my homeland forever.

© OSCAR HAMMERSTEIN II
FROM THE 20TH CENTURY FOX FILM
The Sound of Music

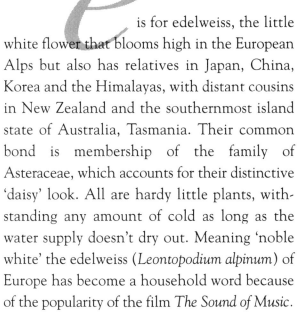

e is for edelweiss, the little white flower that blooms high in the European Alps but also has relatives in Japan, China, Korea and the Himalayas, with distant cousins in New Zealand and the southernmost island state of Australia, Tasmania. Their common bond is membership of the family of Asteraceae, which accounts for their distinctive 'daisy' look. All are hardy little plants, withstanding any amount of cold as long as the water supply doesn't dry out. Meaning 'noble white' the edelweiss (*Leontopodium alpinum*) of Europe has become a household word because of the popularity of the film *The Sound of Music*.

Famed for its ability to survive bitter conditions the edelweiss is the floral emblem of Switzerland. Its leaves are densely covered with white hairs and shaped in a rosette. Within these rosettes are whitish star-shaped flowers which occur in dense, flat-topped clusters like furry daisies.

WORKING NOTES: Pale, nothing-coloured greens express this alpine plant's unassuming nature. The E dominates the flowers in the version at right where I have again used two gold velvets and gold metallic thread. Thread around the flowers is tonally similar to the fabric of petals and background. The other one, where the letter and flower have equal 'billing', is highly illustrative and explains quickly what an edelweiss is. The greens are ghostly, almost luminous, with the purple restrained by stitching in the same colour.

*You may deprive me of anything you like
except coffee, cigarettes and figs.*

PAUL VALÉRY

f is for fig, that rich fruit of the tree thought to have originated in China. Since then it has become one of the four essential foods of Mediterranean people along with olives, grapes and wheat.

The fig tree was almost certainly domesticated in the area of Asia Minor that is now Turkey, but it has been known, written and sung about since ancient times.

When Adam and Eve sought to hide their nakedness in the Garden of Eden, they took fig leaves and made them into skirts. This early association with human nudity has been carried forward over the years so that even today there is still an aura of sensuality about this delightful and mysterious fruit.

Diogenes, the Greek cynic who lived much of his life in a barrel, is recorded as sharing a meal of figs with Plato (who apparently took more than his share) some two thousand years ago.

Today figs can be used in any number of ways from being eaten fresh, cooked as a dessert, dried for later use or even distilled into a spirit.

CARAMEL FIGS
*Dip ripe figs in water then roll thickly
in caster sugar. Pack figs tightly together in
oven-proof dish and bake at 220°C (425°F)
for about 20 minutes. Cool, then chill.
Serve with cream.*

One square = 2.5 centimetres (1 inch)

WORKING NOTES: At left, an autumnal selection of colours contrasts with the steely blue and grey of the initial. The differences between the velvety skin and the jewel-like seeds can be expressed in different fabrics. By altering nap direction, the two shades of pink velvet used for the seed sections 'read' as several different tones. A narrower width for the satin stitch seemed to suit the intricacy of this segment. The other colour way is very bright featuring the vivid biting greens characteristic of green figs.

44

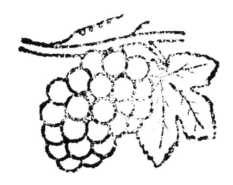

Man, being reasonable, must get drunk;
The best of life is but intoxication:
Glory, the grape, love, gold, in these are sunk
The hopes of all men, and of every nation.

LORD BYRON
Don Juan

g is for grape in all its glorious seasonal colours. Landscapes of vineyards in bright spring green turn into patchworks of gold and brown soon after the grapes are harvested. The intoxicating side effects of fermented grapes were discovered long ago and evidence of the popularity of the grape can be found in early Greek and Roman times in the legends of Dionysus and Bacchus.

It was Dionysus who introduced the cultivation of the vine and he is frequently portrayed with a drinking horn and vine leaves. The Romans knew him as Bacchus, and the 'orgia', the religious rites surrounding Dionysus, became the Roman bacchanalia. Ultimately these revels became uncontrollable forcing the government to pass a law in 186 BC to repress the bacchanalia and its accompanying crime wave.

The depiction of Dionysus has changed over the centuries from a portly bearded man to a handsome youth with flashing eyes and flowing locks.

Wine makes everyone younger – until the following morning.

GRAPE BRÛLÉE
Spread a bunch of seedless grapes evenly on foil and cover with whipped cream.
Sprinkle generously with brown sugar and freeze. When completely frozen, remove from freezer
and place under griller until sugar caramelizes. Serve immediately.

One square = 2.5 centimetres (1 inch)

WORKING NOTES: This is a tricky design because of the control needed to stitch the leaves. To sew it successfully you have to be very well connected to your machine. In the autumnal version, leaves are shades of rust and orange against the green of the juice-laden grapes and entwine around a pink and tan G. The summery one is set on a classic Barbara Cartland pink background. Shades of green in the leaves contrast with muscatel grapes and the letter. In both appliqués, the grapes and leaves are stitched in harmonious tones.

h is for hippeastrum, a native of South America, which has given rise to some exotic hybrids. The name comes from the Greek word 'hippeus' meaning night or stars, seemingly a reference to the distinctive shape of the flowers. One of my favourite flowers, its clean lines and broad shapes lend themselves perfectly to my appliqué technique. Unlike many more intricate blooms, I find it easy to make the shape of the hippeastrum look convincing.

The hippeastrum (also known as the Barbados lily and Peruvian daffodil) is a member of the family Amaryllidaceae as is the belladonna lily with which it is often confused.

Possibly the biggest bloomers in the bulb kingdom and extremely long lasting once bulbs are established, hippeastrums come in fabulous shades of white, gold, scarlet, pink and orange made even richer by velvety textured petals. In some parts of Europe, they are grown in pots on window-sills to present a display of handsome flowers as soon as spring arrives. Because they do not need to be planted very deeply, they are well suited to cultivation in containers for inner city dwellers.

I never cease to wonder at the splendour that explodes from the fist-sized hippeastrum bulb that lies dormant for the winter months and then, like the most elaborate pyrotechnic show, presents a wealth of colour and shape.

One square = 2.5 centimetres (1 inch)

WORKING NOTES: This very simple fleshy image lends itself perfectly to the technique. Keeping to the tones of one colour, interpret the broad shapes of the flowers with a variety of textured fabrics. The H, stem and leaves are constructed in several shades of green velvet. Metallic gold thread around the letter detaches it in a subtle way from the leaves. In the other white version, mix plain and slub weaves with velvet for the flowers. Ringing the changes by means of textural interplay it is at its most alluring in white.

i is for iris from the family Iridaceae. One of the oldest known plants with tuberous roots and showy flowers, it has been closely associated with women through the centuries. Iris, the messenger of the goddess Juno, travelled from heaven to earth and back again on the rainbow to collect the souls of women. To help the soul-gatherer the ancient Greeks planted irises on the graves of women.

Later the Roman historian Plutarch named the iris 'the eye of heaven' because the colours of the rainbow are to be found in the fragile, translucent petals. This may also account for the band of colour surrounding the pupil of the eye being known as the iris.

The French royal coat of arms was originally a field of fleur-de-lis, which were in fact irises and not lilies as is commonly believed. Later, Charles V reduced the number of flowers to three to reflect the Christian Trinity and, in the twentieth century, the fleur-de-lis was adopted as the badge of the Boy Scouts.

Iris florentina is a variety of iris cultivated in Tuscany for the production of orris root powder, which is a fixative used to preserve the scents of potpourris and pomanders.

One of the lesser known uses for the iris was in baby care when North American Indians wrapped their newborn children in the leaves of the plant to prevent dehydration.

One square = 2.5 centimetres (1 inch)

WORKING NOTES: In a difficulty rating out of 10, I would give this one 8. Keep up the revs on the machine when negotiating the bends around the flowers. Both versions are based on real irises. The mauve one (left) has a plummy purple I against another purple with leaves and stems in pale grey-greens. Glittery metallic thread 'lifts' the letter away from its background. The other version is much more flashy – a study in blue and purple with bright peacock blue thread around the navy velvet I.

Japonica glistens like coral in all of
the neighbour gardens.

HENRY REED

j is for japonica, a deciduous shrub which produces sweetly scented
'quince blossom' flowers. These flowers are followed by small rounded yellow fruit which are
also richly perfumed. A native of China and
Japan it must be closely related to the quince as
it mirrors almost all the qualities of that tree.
Japonica is deciduous with prickly branches but
its flowers, which come in apricot, pink, crimson, red and 'quince white', are very hardy and
an excellent choice for floral arrangements. If
placed in water, the buds on the branches will
continue to open for weeks.

The seasonal changes of this classic
shrub are very marked and its graphic forms
and shapes make it an ideal source of inspiration for the artist and designer.

Japonica in all its many guises can be
found throughout Japanese decoration from an
adornment on the the smallest netsuke to a
background on a large folding screen.

One square = 2.5 centimetres (1 inch)

WORKING NOTES: For the pastel version the flowers are five shades of pink in gabardine and shantung and almost shimmer against the lilac 'sky'. Two tones of yellow for the centres are stitched with yellow and white thread; these subtle colour changes produce a slightly fuzzy look. More subtle colour changes between threads for leaves and stems are not critical to the design but do add richness. The other one exhibits an altogether stronger colour choice with yellow centres beaming out of red flowers. An orange border gives the J emphasis.

k is for kumquat from the Rutaceae family, a citrus fruit with leaves very similar to those of the mandarin. This evergreen shrub, a native of China and Japan, is used more for decoration than for its fruit. Because of their proportions, kumquats are ideal in pots, and are frequently shaped into standards. A pair of potted kumquats makes a special statement at the front door. A joy to behold throughout the year, they produce fragrant, white, star-shaped blossom in spring followed by small orange-shaped fruit in autumn.

The fruit of the kumquat are tiny and tart and because of their size and many seeds are rarely eaten straight from the branch. They are, however, frequently used for making jams, jellies and liqueurs.

The quantities of ingredients below may seem excessive but if you have the wherewithal, the result is excellent.

BRANDIED KUMQUATS

Take 4 kg (8 lb) of fruit, 1.5 kg (3 lb) of sugar, 1 litre (2 pints) of water and 1 litre of brandy. Prick fruit all over with skewer. Put sugar and water in a large pan and boil gently until syrup begins to form. Add fruit and boil for one minute. Pack fruit into hot sterilised preserving jars leaving little space between fruit. Pour in brandy to fill halfway up jar then top up with syrup until jar is just overflowing. Seal, leave no air gaps and store in a dark place for about four months before use.

One square = 2.5 centimetres (1 inch)

WORKING NOTES: Gold triumphed yet again in this letter and once more I employed my trusty two-tone formula stitched in metallic gold. I used extremes of orange and yellow for the fruit, grossly overstating the colour case. Although the fruit shapes are different colours, see how I've stitched them all in the same thread making the finished piece look more complex that it actually is. Orange and purple are direct opposites on the colour wheel so it is no surprise that the alternative version is the ultimate exercise in contrast.

l is for lotus, a form of aquatic lily credited with many mystical qualities. Egypt has a sacred lotus which appears as a symbol of power and purity in all the visual arts of that ancient civilisation. Homer writes about the lotus eaters, the Lotophagoi, a fabulous people who live on the lotus fruit which induces a state of dreamy forgetfulness and a desire to live forever in Lotusland. According to Mohammed, a lotus tree stands in the seventh heaven on the right-hand side of the throne of God, giving rise to the Arab belief that the lotus is the queen of flowers.

The East is also rich with lotus culture. The most elegant variety, *Nelumbo nucifera*, magically supports the robust figure of the Lord Buddha as he sits on high, worshipped by millions. Or think of a quiet, misty morning, the only soul in sight a beautiful, young, shaven-headed monk clothed in a saffron robe with a lotus bloom in his begging bowl – a synthesis of flower and faith. Peaceful scenes such as this restore the flagging spirits of travellers and locals alike.

Every part of the plant is edible so lotus eating is not just the stuff of legend. Despite tales of hallucination, it is usually consumed without side effects. Lotus seeds may be eaten raw, boiled or grilled and its roots prepared like celery. In Vietnam lotus seeds are the principal ingredient of a sweet soup while in China and Indonesia the leaves are frequently used as edible wrappings for other food.

One square = 2.5 centimetres (1 inch)

WORKING NOTES: This design almost reads as a landscape (perhaps that should be waterscape) with its sense of perspective. Pure white lotus is the classic symbol of peace and meditation and is my personal choice. A limited number of whites was used in this one and the piece relies very much on the stitching with white thread to define shapes. In the pink, there are more choices of cloth and the stitching is not of such importance as it is in the white, and the greens are tinged with bronze and yellow.

*Faint was the air with the odorous breath
of magnolia blossoms.*

WILLIAM WORDSWORTH

M is for magnolia. Once known as tulip trees, they were renamed by the botanist Linnaeus in honour of a director of the French Botanic Gardens at Montpellier, Pierre Magnol.

The magnificent cupped form of its large blooms is similar to that of the sacred lotus and inspired great reverence from the Chinese who often planted a magnolia tree near a temple. This fulsome flower appears frequently in Chinese decorative arts and may be seen on porcelain, screens, embroideries, carpets and in the tapestries of the Tang dynasty.

Magnolia trees can be either deciduous or evergreen. In the evergreen group there is *Magnolia grandiflora*, famed for its large and abundant creamy white flowers and their gentle lemon perfume. The beauty of all magnolia blooms and the velvet-smooth texture of their petals have been used as a measure of a woman's beauty. In the opening pages of the classic story *Gone With the Wind*, Scarlett O'Hara is described as having magnolia-white skin – 'that skin so prized by Southern women and so carefully guarded with bonnets, veils and mittens against hot Georgia suns'.

The magnolia is very much the emblem of the deep south with the state of Mississippi being known as the Magnolia State.

I have chosen to use the deciduous Chinese variety in my design overleaf because the starkness of twigs and buds accentuates the voluptuous blooms.

72

One square = 2.5 centimetres (1 inch)

WORKING NOTES: A mix of white and shades of port wine captures the impression of the magnolia flower. Buds and branches are pussy willow colours with pattern coming from two different neck tie fabrics for the M and part of the border. The whole effect is rather dark and brooding. The other is an off-beat colour combination with the white-on-white flower placed against shot Thai silk of peacock blue with a pink sheen. Stitching of the M is so subtle it makes your teeth ache; two greens with a slightly lighter tone inside.

$\mathcal{N}$ is for nasturtium, a versatile and hardy garden plant that seems to thrive on neglect. Imported to Spain from the Americas it soon became known as Indian cress because it had much of the peppery taste of watercress.

The nasturtium is a very hardy, sun-loving plant which flowers profusely. It can be planted almost anywhere to provide a bright splash of colour in poor soil and even in building rubble. It has many uses as a companion plant and acts as a deterrent to garden pests. Nasturtiums, it is claimed, will help and be helped if they are planted with or near chives and apples.

All these attributes and it is edible as well! Chemists calculate that the leaves contain ten times the amount of vitamin C found in a lettuce. You can use every part of the nasturtium; the flowers for decoration, the succulent leaves in salads, and the seeds are perfect for pickling.

NASTURTIUM AND MARIGOLD SPREAD
(Marigold and nasturtium leaves share a slightly peppery flavour)
120 g (4 oz) unsalted butter, 2 tablespoons of marigold petals, pinch of ground cinnamon, squeeze of lemon juice, bread, nasturtium leaves. Blend butter with marigold petals and cinnamon and add lemon to taste. Spread on bread and cover with nasturtium leaves.

One square = 2.5 centimetres (1 inch)

WORKING NOTES: Nasturtium flowers are so distinctive there seems little point in tampering with nature's palette. At left, the front flower has four different yellow fabrics with four shades of burnt orange for the bloom in profile above it. Leaf veins present a nice pattern in the background, which I have emphasised with stitching. The design is simple to construct and sew; just keep swinging the work around when you stitch the petals' curves. The red version is much stronger because I have contrasted the flowers and leaves against the purple N.

Blonde Aphrodite rose up excited,
Moved to delight by the melody,
White as an orchid she rode quite naked
In an oyster shell on top of the sea.

W. H. Auden
Anthem for St Cecilia's Day

Vanilla Sugar

Place a vanilla bean in an airtight container
with your regular supply of caster sugar and leave
for two weeks. Hey presto – vanilla sugar!
Use it in desserts or as a sprinkling on tea cakes
instead of icing (powdered) sugar.

O is for orchid, the exotic and sometimes intoxicatingly fragrant flower of the tropics. Legends attribute to them medicinal properties both curative and aphrodisiacal and the ability to devour insects, and even humans. None of this is true of course but people are always willing to believe things that are exotic and unlikely. In fact orchids are one of the largest families of flowering plants, found practically everywhere; in the tropics from mountaintop to sea level, in desert sands and close to the ice caps of the arctic.

The Mexican orchid, *Vanilla planifolia*, bears vanilla beans which are flavourless until fermented. It was recorded that when the Aztec Emperor Montezuma drank a cup of chocolate it was flavoured with vanilla.

Mostly, the orchid was sought for its exotic blooms. In fact in the nineteenth century the craze for orchids was so great that plant hunters scoured the world for rare species, which were valued more highly than gold.

One square = 2.5 centimetres (1 inch)

WORKING NOTES: The silvery blue embossed velvet behind the letter was cut in random directions to vary the fabric's shimmering pattern. Using nine different threads seems crazy on reflection but I wanted to give the stronger colours tonal complexity in my representation of a *Cattleya* orchid. Both versions are similar but the O at right is outlined by silver moiré thread. Although the shapes look daunting this is a simple design with fewer pieces than the nasturtiums. Just put your foot down when sewing the wavy bits of the flower.

Take all the sweetness of a gift unsought
And for the pansies send me back a thought.

Sarah Doudney

P is for pansy, the *Viola tricolor*, also known as love-in-idleness and as heartsease. The pansy can frequently be found wild in the northern hemisphere but is mainly known as a domesticated plant. In the wild its flowers are small but when cultivated they become large and variously coloured.

In Shakespeare's play *A Midsummer Night's Dream*, Oberon tells the story of how the pansy acquired its colours. According to legend, Cupid's arrow missed its mark and fell upon a little milk-white flower. The wound from the arrow of love was purple, and the juice that flowed was said to have magical properties and the flower became purple and white. The juice of the pansy was supposed to ease the pains of love, and hence the name heartsease.

The pansy has been recorded since Elizabethan times and appears on a set of tapestries woven around 1500 and now exhibited at the Cloisters Museum in New York. The pansy was also popular with the working class at the start of the Industrial Revolution. To remind them of their origins, many of the uprooted country folk took to growing pansies in the gardens of their tiny terrace houses. The exotic shrubs and other species introduced to Britain in this period were either too costly or too fragile to grow in such bleak conditions, but the humble pansy thrived. Known also as the harlequins or clowns of the garden, the pansy flower will create a festive display for much of the year.

Ring o' Pansies
Fill a ring cake tin with water and pansy flowers and freeze.
Remove from tin and use as a decorative cooler in a punch bowl for summer drinks.

One square = 2.5 centimetres (1 inch)

WORKING NOTES: About 5 on the degree of difficulty scale because it really doesn't really matter if you make a few slips with this one. A mistake makes it look more handmade and adds a bit of integrity to the work. I've chosen to make this appliqué a study of yellow and purple pansies with little white centres surrounding a pale green P. The other colour way is principally purple and uses a lot of satins and shiny fabrics. Velvet was reserved for the dark gold P. Two threads, matched to centres and petals, were selected for the flowers.

88

They dined on mince, and slices of quince,
Which they ate with a runcible spoon;
And hand in hand, on the edge of the sand,
They danced by the light of the moon.

EDWARD LEAR
The Owl and the Pussy-cat

Q is for quince, the fruit of love said to have arrived in Europe from the exotic East with Aphrodite, her arms full of roses. Legend claims that the voluptuous form of the fruit imitates the breasts of this goddess of love. Romantics insist that the narcissus-like fragrance of its blossoms heralds the beginning of love.

Pale yellow in colour, this lustrous fruit would seem to have the credentials to be recognised as the 'Close bosom-friend of the maturing sun'.

Perhaps it could even become the botanic symbol of the 'Season of mists and mellow fruitfulness'.

QUINCE VODKA
Scrub and clean two good-sized quinces.
Grate them completely including skins and cores.
Place result into a sterilised 1 litre bottling jar.
Add 60 g (2 oz or a quarter cup) of caster sugar.
Fill jar to the top with vodka (gin will also serve),
close tightly and store in a dark place for at least
six months. Strain off resulting liquid into
a clean bottle and label suitably.

WORKING NOTES: Because of its big, broad, bold shapes this is probably the simplest design in the collection. The fruit seem to glow, almost pulsate, when stitched with lighter coloured threads. The leaves are also stitched in bronze thread instead of a perfect match. In the other colour way, the pinky version, I used metallic copper thread around the letter Q. The little signature square, which is often found in the narrow border, offers a jewel of colour in the far corner of the design.

The rose by any other name would smell as sweet.

SHAKESPEARE
Romeo and Juliet

r is for rose, surely the most popular flower in the world. From Robert Herrick's admonishment to 'Gather ye rose-buds while ye may' to Gertrude Stein's facetious line that a 'Rose is a rose is a rose', the rose has been a favoured literary subject for centuries.

Rosaries were originally made with compressed rose petals, which gave off a perpetual fragrance. Many of our everyday expressions include the word rose. Typical is the term 'sub rosa', whereby meetings held beneath a suspended rose are deemed to be under an oath of secrecy. One explanation goes back to the fifth century BC to secret talks held by the Greeks in a rose bower. They had been defeated on land by Xerxes and gathered to plan a counter attack at sea. Another expression 'a bed of roses' has its origins in Roman times, when Nero's banqueting hall was strewn with roses and guests rested on rose-filled cushions.

To Make Rosewater

Gather red roses when they are full-blown and, measuring 10 litres as densely as possible in a 1 litre container (or similar as long as the final quantity is the same), put them in a large boiler with approximately 1 litre of cold water. Heat very gently for 45 minutes, stirring occasionally and never allowing the water to boil. Leave the resulting essence overnight in a covered container and strain into opaque airtight bottles.

One square = 2.5 centimetres (1 inch)

WORKING NOTES: The letter, a major contributor to the design's richness, is cut from a subtly watermarked deep rose-red velvet and sewn in thread to match. An unusual choice of pale sea green for the thread around the leaves gives a slightly luminous effect. However, in this version, the yellow blooms attract the most attention. At right, the green and gold R is dominant with its outer rim 'etched' with gold metallic thread. Notice how the sewing of the R spills out into the corner beyond the letter.

S is for *Strelitzia reginae*, a species of herbaceous plant that was named after Charlotte of Mecklenburg-Strelitz (wife of George III – hence the *reginae*). Native to South Africa, the striking strelitzia flower (opposite), which is also known as the bird of paradise or crane flower, has been adopted as the floral emblem of both the province of Natal in South Africa and the city of Los Angeles in the USA.

The plant has blade-like leaves with the flowers rising majestically from spathes supported by long thick stems. Botanically, the strelitzia is a glamorous relative of the more humble banana, which goes to prove that there are high flyers in every family.

The flower of *S. reginae* is like an answer to an artist's prayer. Not only is it very graphic in line and form but it also presents a collection of brilliant clashing shades of orange, red and fluorescent blues and purples. All this is played out against a thicket of silver green paddle-shaped leaves. No wonder the strelitzia became the style emblem of the heady 1980s. It could be said that the strelitzia was to that decade what the nasturtium was to the art nouveau movement of the late nineteenth century.

Another interesting plant is *Ravenala madagascariensis* or traveller's tree (above), of the same family, Strelitziaceae. This can grow to a height of 10 m with white petals on huge flower heads six times the size of its more ostentatious but smaller relative.

WORKING NOTES: So it can survive the colour battle, the vividly outlined S is a stark contrast to the flowers. Unusual slubby silks were used in the nothing green foliage. See how the orange bronze of the petals is echoed in the bottom left signature square. The other one is what I call the Florida Keys colouration with the yellow-edged S taking a lesser role in the overall design. Because I lost some of the cut pieces, two different plum fabrics appear behind the letter. Having a perfect match is not essential; it doesn't matter a damn.

it was as true … as turnips is. It was as true …
as taxes is. And nothing's truer than them.

CHARLES DICKENS
David Copperfield

t is for turnip, a humble vegetable as honest as the potato. Consider its attributes. It is cheap, nutritious, filling, low in kilojoules (calories) and high in carbohydrate; all excellent assets in times of financial hardship. The turnip is an excellent vegetable, and its decline is to be mourned.

In its heyday, the turnip constituted a major part of the Roman diet, and the Romans introduced it to many parts of their empire. In 1539, long after the decline and fall, Sir Thomas Elyot wrote that boiled turnips were not only nourishing but that they 'augmented the sede of man' and 'provoketh carnell lust' – pretty good for a vegetable that is 90% water.

Turnips are easy to grow, take up very little space and the young tops can even be used in cooking. Make a nourishing bright green soup with the turnip tops cooked lightly with butter, spring onions, a little sorrel, parsley and stock. The 'garnish' consists of peeled and boiled turnips mashed with cream and this purée is swirled into the centre of each bowl.

Because turnips are good absorbers of fat, they are traditionally served with very fatty meats such as mutton or duck.

TOFFEED TURNIPS
Take 500 g (1 lb) of turnips, peel thickly
and dice into 10 mm ($^1/_2$ in) squares. Boil in salted
water until tender. Drain. Melt nob of butter
in a pan, stir in 1 tablespoon of honey and a few
grinds of nutmeg and sauté on low heat
for about 1 minute.

One square = 2.5 centimetres (1 inch)

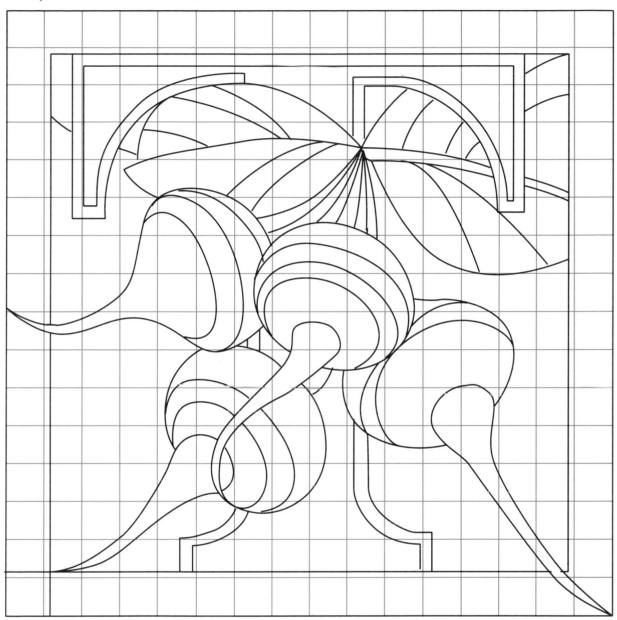

WORKING NOTES: This is a favourite image of mine developed some time ago for an appliqué mural now owned by a firm of fruit and vegetable wholesalers. It is simple to vary shapes slightly and alter colours in order to change the vegetables to beetroots or radishes. Both the vegetables and the T have equal impact and in this one I used a number of different threads with the leaves sewn in one colour and the turnips in three others. The alternate version is much more festive with metallic thread on the T.

The rain, it raineth on the just
And also on the unjust fella:
But chiefly on the just, because
The unjust steals the just's umbrella.

LORD BOWEN

U is for the umbrella tree and tell me pray what other suitable plant or flower starts with the letter U? Originally from China, the germinated seeds slowly spread down through Indonesia to Australia where the tree now grows naturally in the remaining coastal rainforests of the eastern states. The umbrella tree's flowers are red clusters like brilliant popcorn stuck to the ribs of an umbrella. *Schefflera actinophylla* is also known as the octopus tree because of the shape of these flowers but we shall not dwell on this other name since it was hard enough to find a suitable subject for U in the first place.

An umbrella has been aptly described as 'a defence against rain, now usually of silk, alpaca etc., fastened on slender ribs which are attached radially to a stick and can be readily raised so as to form a circular arched canopy'. Perfect!

The design, which was originally developed as a protection against the sun, has remained unchanged for thousands of years. Looking at an umbrella tree from a practical point of view, it could be said that here is a perfect case of nature following art.

When the composer Erik Satie died in Paris in 1925 over 200 umbrellas were found in his apartment.
See Lord Bowen's dictum at the top of this page.

One square = 2.5 centimetres (1 inch)

WORKING NOTES: This study in greens exhibits many shades of the colour we all associate with 'go' and 'grow'. From the acid green of the letter to the softest olives of the leaves the only really outstanding colour feature here is the pale, sea-green stitching of the U. Perspective has been attempted in the brown and blue version by making the leaves behind the U darker and lifting the foreground with lighter colours. Gold metallic thread defines the linear elements of the letter.

I shall return in the spring with the violets.

Napoleon Bonaparte

V is for violet, once the symbol of the city of Athens, the flower that entwined Napoleon and Josephine and the most adored flower in Victorian England. Shakespeare wrote of violets in many of his plays and in *Hamlet* he described the elusive nature of their perfume – 'The perfume and suppliance of a minute, no more'. This observation is particularly telling as later scientific studies have shown that the principal ingredient of the violet's aroma, ionine, quickly stifles our sense of smell so that the fragrance seems to fade rapidly.

Napoleon's Empress Josephine had violets embroidered on her wedding gown. Later, the word violet was used as a code word to identify the faithful during Napoleon's banishment on Elba. For the rest of his life after Josephine's death, Napoleon wore a locket containing a violet from her grave.

For many years violets were thought to have medicinal properties capable of suppressing inflammation of the lungs and even today some Europeans believe that eating violet leaves will arrest the spread of cancer.

Violet Soufflé

Prepare a dessert soufflé mixture and flavour it with 5–6 drops of essence of violets before folding in the stiffly whisked egg whites. Add a dozen chopped crystalised violets and complete the soufflé in the usual manner. Place a posy of fresh violets beside the soufflé when serving.

One square = 2.5 centimetres (1 inch)

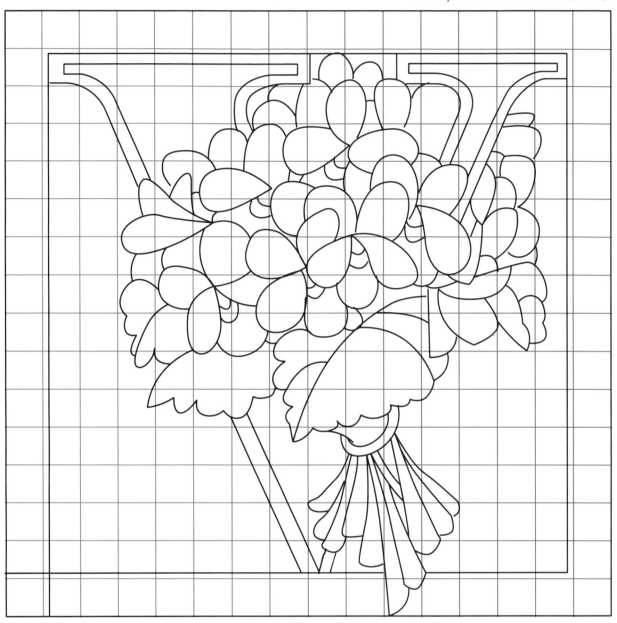

WORKING NOTES: Looks hard but isn't – another 5 on the degree of difficulty scale because all the pieces are massed and the satin stitch can disguise errors in cutting and placement. For the flowers, use lots of purples, blacks, navy blues and violets. My selection of several shades of green for the background conjures up the antique atmosphere of an old lady's bedroom. Petals in the other one were stitched in purple metallic, which adds glitter and dimension. The pale gold V stands out on the background of patterned woven tie fabric.

Rödnäckros

Nymphaea alba   *f. rosea*

Sverige 3 50

AXELSSON

L.S sc

W is for waterlily, the all-purpose name used to describe several species of flowering plant of the *Nymphaea* genus, so called because it was found naturally in environments reputedly inhabited by water nymphs, who camouflaged themselves with lily blooms to elude the advances of their menfolk.

As they float on the surface of a lake, waterlilies provide a natural focus for meditation, peace and tranquillity. They are the symbol of purity.

Waterlilies open their flowers with the dawn and close them naturally with the setting sun. The ancient Egyptians associated the time cycle of the waterlily with Osiris, the god of the dead, who represented reincarnation and thereby, eternal life. The waterlily demonstrated this renewal perfectly.

The painter Claude Monet was so fascinated by the waterlilies that he grew in his lake at Giverney that he spent many years of his life recording them in every light and at every stage of their development.

The habit of closing their petals as the evening draws nigh means that waterlilies are less than ideal in a floral arrangement. However, if you are determined to display these magnificent aquatic blooms on some special occasion, a blob of candle wax dropped between the petals will keep them open all night long.

WORKING NOTES: Flower and leaves form another waterscape with perspective and strong imagery. In the version at right the flower is the ultimate study in whites and creams with a classic gold W contrasting with the background. The W in the blue rendition is held back by a background of equal richness and strength. The star of this piece is the crimson waterlily. Both versions are acceptable botanically but don't ever let this hold you back. Some of my colour choices are quite outrageous.

X is for xanthorrhea the beautiful grass tree. Its name hints at a connection with Xanadu but Coleridge didn't mention it in his famous poem *Kubla Khan*. An oversight perhaps? In fact grass trees are natives of south-eastern Australia and Tasmania but are exotic enough to have graced the fictional 'stately pleasure-dome'.

Appropriately enough members of the genus *Xanthorrhea*, or blackboys as they are more commonly called, are slow to grow and often take ten years or more to reach maturity. The trunk of the shrub is short and rough with leaves that are stiff and grassy. Out of this grassy topknot projects a spear-like stem which, when in bloom, is covered with masses of tiny white flowers. After the flowers are finished, they drop away leaving the tall chocolate brown phallus for another year.

Early colonial artists working in Australia often included xanthorrheas in their drawings. Usually they were combined with kangaroos, emus and Aborigines to convey a bizarre impression of this newly discovered land. One well-known etching that depicts the genocide of the indigenous people of Van Diemen's Land by the British militia has the background liberally covered with these odd looking plants. Another shows an English settler's cottage garden with a picket fence beyond which lurk more of these spectacular shrubs to contrast the tame with the wild.

Hopefully, future generations will stop using xanthorrhea's common name, a sad legacy of colonial times, and this pre-historic grass tree will be known by its more democratic and interesting botanical name.

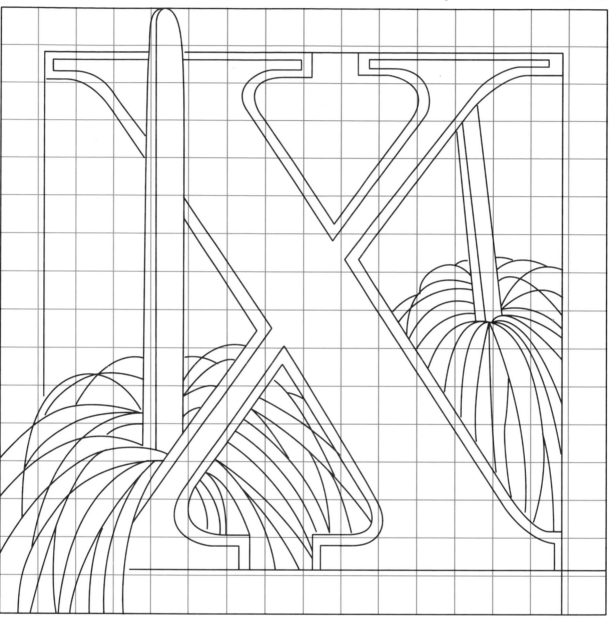

WORKING NOTES: A 6 on my difficulty scale, this design is very easy to sew. The hardest part is dealing with the letter X with its flapping thin 'arms' that resist control at the cutting, spraying and pasting-into-position stages. The outer borders of the letter are particularly tiresome. Burgundy velvet background has its sections cut in random directions for nap variations. The other one is influenced by earth colours. Although they are known as blackboys, there is no black in the spear portion, only in the X of the one at right.

Y is for the yucca plant, *Yucca filamentosa*, also sometimes known as Adam's needle. Notorious for remaining flowerless for years on end, it can be sensational when it does eventually bloom.

A possible explanation for its reticence is that the yucca is a desert dweller and therefore more comfortable blooming when harsh, dry conditions prevail. Some home gardeners advise digging a trench around the plant to reveal its roots, then covering the exposed parts with rocks, stones and a shallow layer of soil; a somewhat drastic way to create a desert environment for what may still be triennial blooms.

Giant yuccas reaching enormous heights grow in the western Mojave Desert in the USA at altitudes exceeding 1500 m (4650 ft). They were often called Joshua trees, because the early pioneers thought that they resembled the prophet Joshua waving the thirsty travellers towards the Promised Land. East of Los Angeles, a Joshua Tree National Monument commemorates this fable.

The yucca has a unique partnership with the female yucca moth. Moth and plant are mutually dependent. The moth has special organs with which to collect and distribute the pollen from the flowers of one yucca plant to another. In return, the moth lays its eggs on the flower which conveniently provides food for the young.

ND FRUTICETUM.

have had any account of, either at home or abroad. There are plants, both of this variety and of the species, in the Horticultural Society's Garden, in the Epsom Nursery, and at Messrs. Loddiges's

One square = 2.5 centimetres (1 inch)

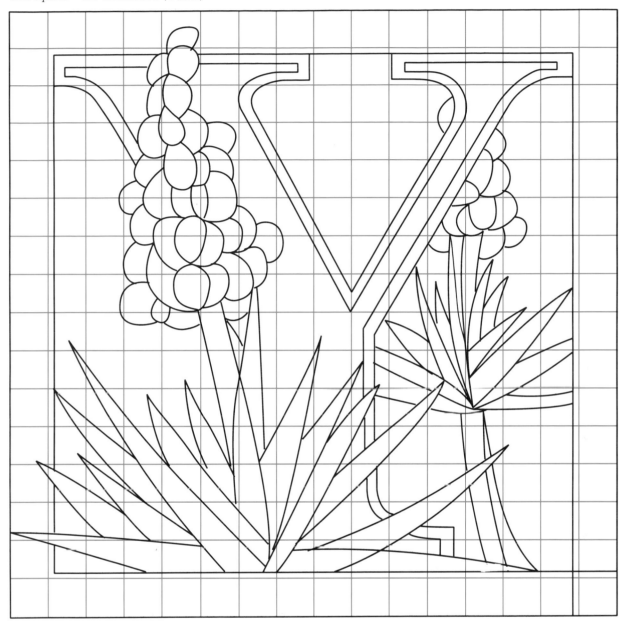

WORKING NOTES: To highlight these huge and intriguing plants create a muted outdoor look with gold and blue that is both dramatic and closely related to nature. The brown version is a more graphic, stylised treatment with earth colours of tan, deep gold, burnt sienna and Venetian red. Scale of difficulty is about a 7 – to disguise imperfections you can oversew the yucca until your thread supply runs out. In both versions, the plant at back has a subtle change of thread colour to suggest distance.

Z is for zinnia of course. Cultivated by the ancient Aztecs together with dahlias, sunflowers and the ubiquitous morning glory, how disappointing that it is not named after Montezuma or the quetzal. Instead it honours a certain Gottfried Zinn. This gentleman, a professor of botany at the University of Göttingen, received some of the first seeds to reach Europe in the eighteenth century from his friend, the German ambassador to Mexico. This timely gift ultimately propelled the name Zinn into posterity.

Zinnia elegans is one of the better known of several varieties of this popular, sun-loving annual. Used in parks and gardens for spectacular borders of vivid massed colour, the zinnia is also a long-term favourite of the home gardener. For balcony gardeners, dwarf varieties perform very well in containers.

The leaves and stem of this plant are a soft delicate green and strangely furry to the touch. Zinnias come in vibrant shades of rose, pink, lilac, crimson, scarlet, red and orange as well as white. Recently a new and very exotic chartreuse-coloured strain, green envy, has been introduced.

So simple is the zinnia that its form could have come from a child's drawing – a stick-like stem, a few leaves and a big blob of colour on top with a yellow dot in the middle.

One square = 2.5 centimetres (1 inch)

WORKING NOTES: For the red and yellow version (left) I've thrown in as many different reds as I could find and chosen two different reds to stitch the Z. Purple makes a token appearance in the background's crimson zinnia, the signature square and the stem of the front flower. A handsome black version gives more power to the letter, which is edged in bronze silk and stitched with khaki thread. The interesting piece of patterned rust red and black velvet is a buffer between the cushion's edge and the colour zone.